CW00621567

The KALEIDOSCOPE of TIME

The publishers are grateful to Faber and Faber for their kind permission to reproduce lines from T. S. Eliot's 'Four Quartets'.

The Kaleidoscope of Time

Stacey International
128 Kensington Church Street
London W8 4BH
Tel: +44 (0)20 7221 7166 Fax: +44 (0)20 7792 9288
www.stacey-international.co.uk

© India Russell 2007

ISBN: 978-1905299-52-2

CIP Data: A catalogue record for this book is available
from the British Library

Printed and bound in Great Britain by
Biddles of King's Lynn, Norfolk

The KALEIDOSCOPE of TIME

India Russell

STACEY
INTERNATIONAL

ACKNOWLEDGEMENTS

Acknowledgements are due to the editors of *Acumen, Dream Catcher, Pulsar, Roundyhouse, The Swansea Review* and *Temenos Academy Review* in which some of these poems were first published.

CONTENTS

THE KALEIDOSCOPE OF TIME

~~~

The Unknowable Essence of Change

All things change, the note cannot be held
The lineaments of beauty fade and blur
The flint edge rounds
The loved home loses its inhabitants,
Falls into neglect
                  and disintegrates
Into the particles that once made up its glory.

All things change;
Yet from this moving symphony
There suddenly arises an abiding tone,
A time-denying note, which
Quires to Heaven singing of realms unknown,
Beautiful and everlasting but, as yet, uncomprehended.

~~~

Once Upon a Time

And the willows wept

Long, long ago when Alice and Ratty and Mole lived in this lovely
land
And willows wept not for sadness but joy at their pure reflections,

and the old overmantle mirrored a world
where God in His Heaven ordained All to be Right
and a boy in a sailor suit, as befitted a young
English gentleman, seen but not heard by visiting great-aunts
sitting out their stay, belaced, cameoed and staid
amongst the unshockable furniture and the hissing
gas lamps remembering Flanders' invisible, unmentionable
dead,

Gods still visited the Earth, married mortals
Begat joyful, impossible children
Who ran amok, crying of Beauty and Truth
Gathering wide-eyed followers.

And the little sailor grew towards manhood
Sensing his wonderful kinship
And ran away, not to sea but in mind
Dreaming a Spiritual Dance
Where he and his Movement
Would combat misuse of science, power politics
And greed and all would be Beauty and Truth
Over the whole divine earth

but the old overmantle still
mirrored an unshakeable world
while Flanders' dead festered.

And for a few light years he ecstatically carried the beacon of
Truth, the halo of Beauty.

Then came the visible, unavoidable war
And the bare-footed dreamers danced on, feet bleeding
Not knowing the gods had despaired of the race
As politics became power, science a weapon
And Greed the new deity.

But when in the blast the old overmantle crashed to the floor
And the unshakeable furniture lost its secure reflection
The divine dancers ceased
Visions darkened to myth
And the willows shook wildly, weeping into quiet poisoned
streams,
Wept for their young, innocent protégé continuing, unsung,
his tragic journey on earth
While the bombs dropped on London and Dresden and the
beautiful gods.

Once Upon a Time

Tell me a story, Grandpa.

Once upon a time . . .
The walls moved in to listen
And the leaping flames illumined
Fairy lanes and meadows,
Witches' cottages,
A magic bean stalk
That led up
Beyond the clouds
Into a castle
Where I hid beneath
A table like a ship,
Terrified of giant footfalls,
'Fi, fy, fo, fum,
I smell the blood of an
Englishman.
Be he alive or be he dead
I'll . . . '

But those are Grandpa's feet
And that's <u>his</u> voice and twinkling eyes
And there is Nanna knitting,
Smiling down at me.
Oh . . . I'll climb just one more
Time and steal the
Golden harp
And then we all can
Live together
Happily by the fire

With Nanna knitting,
Me upon the mat,
Grandpa wearing friendly slippers, snug in his armchair,
Mummy, Daddy and the baby safe at
Home
And everything that's horrid
Far away
For ever and ever after.

Tell me a story, Grandpa.

The Ritual

Jump-walking down the warm, familiar street,
The grinning cracks all waiting to devour me,
I note, with due solemnity, the ritual of the stages:
The house that has a writhing jungle at its towering windows,
The house with nothing in it but a great piano and no one
Ever playing, and then, oh horror, I take
My mother's hand, the house that has The Head –
There behind the window, on the sill, its glinting eyes still
Staring at the street, its long grey-yellow haired
Moustaches so like my terrifying grandfather's in
Wimbledon, (I have to look or else it all is spoiled),
The grey, great curtains and the gaping room;
We manage to pass by;
Then the house that hides behind the dark and dusty hedge,
                                        then I jump,
And just in time, two massive cracks, the Yawning Giant ones,
And then, relief, the gleaming steps into
The House of Books.

Silly school behind me, teeming evening still ahead,
I climb up to the doors, a lone Princess.
Smiling, my mother shows me where to go, (I'd known
Already for an eager week). And solemnly I enter,
Through the little gate, The Junior Library.

And there, all round me, rows and rows of books
All full of boys and girls and animals and magic islands,
Fairies who will lend me wings – all friends
Who'll let me share their midnight feasts
And journeys into fairyland
And I'll be one of them and play and laugh and fly

And I'll be safe
From all the grinning cracks and giants and glinting, glassy eyes
That wait outside the school gates to devour me.

The Guest

My Uncle George, a quiet and thinking man
      Lived in a gypsy caravan.
He'd had enough of life as it is lived
And so, retiring from the fray,
           began to live.

He walked all round the ruggèd coasts of Britain
      Pausing, not to photograph
Or write but just to ponder and to think
And dwell upon the strange phenomenon
           of man.

He was at home with flowers and with birds
      And listened with great knowledge to
The wind and rain and sighings of the planet
And so his story was to him
           not strange.

By way of land-rent for his caravan
      He tended vegetables and fruit
And, sometimes, when the farmer was not resident
Lived in as keeper of his ancient,
           knowing home.

And, he told me, often he was there
      In that so isolated house
The creaking casements singing to the wind
The hushing Surrey countryside stretching
           far around.

Only his twenty cats who formed his bed-cover
      Would visit him and then return
To his warm caravan that was their home
And Uncle George would sit on by the
                leaping fire.

But rarely, so he said, was he alone.
      A man would suddenly appear
And sit down in that other fireside chair
And nod at him and seem at home
              and both would be content.

And after a while my Uncle George would stir
      And say to him, 'Good evening',
And the ghost, for ghost it was,
Would not reply but seem relaxed and pleased to be
              in his dear company.

And when I asked him if he had been afraid
      For I was only young, he said,
Surprised, 'Oh, no! He was a friendly soul
Unlike those city spectres I chose to leave.
              He was my guest.'

Whidown, near Paradise, England

It's the bloody I.R.A.!
My father, rushing down in afternoon pyjamas
To the cold store,
Where the ginger beer had Irishly exploded.

Strange to think that
Whidown, so remote
That my parents used an
Ordnance Survey number
On their visiting cards,
Could be thought of as a target,
Even in my father's haunted mind.

But then, with so much
Tumult in our family,
My father's and my uncle's *Bureau of Spiritual Advice*
'Aiming to create a New World Order' (before they
                both had married and knew better)
'with pamphlets, talks and organised discussions
in Wimbledon and environs',
My theatre and its serious productions that
Would change the world,
My brother's shattering and innocent
Death within
A car crash, that did change our world but not as we
                                had planned,
my father
having to identify the body,
The drinking and the desperation
And no amelioration,

11

It would be more in
Keeping with the terrible fates
For the I.R.A. to cause a threatening
Explosion down at Whidown,
Rather than the home-made ginger beer.

The Lost Loppers

'He left them somewhere
In the orchard, when he was pruning,
The damnfool, useless gardener!'

They'll be rusting now in all that long grass
But I'll search and find them;
Perhaps they're in the loose box;
Or the fruit shed; not the garden room.
He wouldn't go in there. I'll find the loppers,
I think in half-sleep.
I'll wear wellingtons and take a scythe.
I wonder if the stream is full
Or just a trickle. It's like
A fairyland in Spring
Beneath the little bridge
With flowers growing down the banks
Gazing in their watercoloured mirror
The massy rhododendrons standing
Guard before the woods.
I'm sure I'll find them . . .

And then I wake up
To the fact that no one cares
About the silly loppers
Apart from my sad, dreaming self.

There is no family home now,
My father ill in Africa,
My mother following my brother
Beyond life.

Only I am here, in England,
Worrying about Whidown,
The long-grass in the orchard
And the rusting tools.

Man and Nature

Apollo's Ghost

The sun comes up to silence,
Remembering with searing sorrow,
How, as Apollo, his glorious arrival
Drew jubilant chorus from the springing world

But now, unable to arise
From its poor poisoned bed,
The world moves only slightly, as at a half-remembered,
golden dream,
Then sinks back into dying resignation.

Neighbours

I wanted you to be the first to know,
The man from next door said.
What! Was his barren-looking wife
Alive with life!
Stranger things have happened, I suppose;
The dead have risen from the grave
And Hermione was not a statue
After all.
But for a waxwork, who kept
Two dogs, locked up,
To suddenly be fertile, was
A stunning thought.

Oh. Yes, I said, imagining horse-powered buggies.
Yes! I've sold the car, the neighbour said and went quite white.
A wrench, he winced.
It must have been, I thought.
The time he spent embracing
That low deafening weapon
Which punctuates our lives in antiphon with the dogs,
He must have formed a physical bond
And probably now was bleeding.

Should I call a doctor?
She wouldn't notice. Waxworks don't.
I smiled
And mumbled a congratulatory phrase, trying to
Remember where we kept
The First Aid box.

Can I get you anything . . .
Whisky? some Elastoplast?

I'm afraid my wife's away.
She usually does the cleaning up . . .
I mean . . . the entertaining.
He laughed.
Yes quite a wrench a whisky would be fine.

Perhaps he'd dab it on the wound.
We drank and smiled.
That's better. I hope you're
Enjoying yours?
My what? My wife? A bit
Familiar when one's only met in
Argument.
I see you've got a new car.
Oh yes, I said, enlightened. Yes,
Yes. Rust, you know.

Ah. Rust. Well thanks I'd
Better go and break the news to
Sean and Jane.
Oh. Yes, I said. And thanks
For coming round.
That's OK s'what friends
Are for. He turned
And limped
Into the dusk,
Blood dripping, like dark oil stains,
On the drive.

Tavistock Square in April

Interviewer: What do you think of Western Civilisation?
Gandhi: I think it would be a good idea.

London's traffic roars its ugly way
Around the peaceful square
While headlines shout of violence, revolution, horror,
Murderous religions. Assassination.
'Human Head Found in Shark!'
Gasp shocked and moral newspapers.

Sharks' fins, lambs' poor, butchered bodies
Found in humans, mourns Mahatma Gandhi's spirit
In the holy centre of the square
Where worshipping tulips bend bright loving-cups
Towards his bowed and gentle form,
Forget-me-nots whispering at his feet,
Forget me not!

Do not forget that greed and violence
In all its gross and subtle forms destroys the spirit.
Do not forget.
Remember. Walk the way of loving peace. Do not forget.

The listening pigeons coo and peacefully walk
Amongst the falling cherry blossom
                    falling from the sad memorial tree to Hiroshima
                    and civilisation's guilt.

But still the angry traffic bullies on
And headlines shout their papers' popular wares of
Massacres, and revolution, horror. 'Pictures!', they cry.
'Full details!' – Come buy! Come buy!

Do not forget, sighs Gandhi's great soul in the flowering square,
    the animal's bright innocence
    the great tree's healing shade.
Hold back the butchering blade.
Do not forget
    Flanders and

    Dresden

    London

    Auschwitz

    Hiroshima

Do not forget

Do not forget

The Raggèd Crow

I don't want to know about your private life
Or pry into your mind
Or think about the long, lean years and petty persecutions
That have left you raggèd and alone.

I only want to thank you
For your ancient outline on the
Rooves at dusk,
Your stoic flight
And powerful, primæval voice.

I only want to say that I, a
Raggèd fellow being, gain strength
From your ingression in my life
And think of you as I stand
Here
With flowing love
      Whose source must surely be a heavenly spring
      That binds us closer far than any blood.

Soul Mates

We're not really suited,
No literary tastes in common,
Haven't seen the latest exhibitions.
It's true we've both been
Separated, lost our mates,
But that is no excuse
Or explanation
For the thrill that sparks
Our meeting in the morning,
I in my old dressing gown
And he well-spruced and ready for the day.

The link between us hums,
Is so compelling
That I'm lost and cannot start my work
Until I see him, waiting for me,
Sturdy and supporting and saying nothing.

But we really are not suited (in the common sense)
The woodpigeon and I.

War Time Memories

It was a terrible time to raise a family.

Day-time raids and later
Night raids,
Sudden sickening attacks,
Our love-nest, babies, all, destroyed;
And then the long, laborious task
Of finding yet another home,
Building, stick by stick, a safer
Place to rear our precious brood - and still
The need for constant vigilance,
Honed sensitivity to every threatening noise,
The siren warnings sounding constantly,
Impossibility of rest.
At any time of day those sly, winged missiles,
Plunging from the sky,
Could blast our homes apart
Or even worse, at night, in silence, dreadful
Creeping terrorists could
Slink from murky ambushes and murder on the run.

We counter-attacked of course,
By air,
Our small black craft so frail
                against the blazing fighters;
But on the ground we had no chance
Beside that grey, sleek, green-eyed army.

But now it's past, there is a breathing space,
The victims all at rest,
Their rain-soaked, ransacked homes
Returning now to Nature
                    while kindly Autumn watches
As our two miraculous offspring we managed to
Protect, bounce, strong and confident,
Across the grass – the apple
Of their mother's eye.

Oh, yes, it was a terrible time for blackbirds,
This bursting, treacherous Spring.

The Caged Bird

to William Blake and Thomas Hardy

If singing could break bars
He would be free

Free to join his cousins
In the scented air
Or navigate the sky roads flowing home
Free to glide and swoop and turn
And drift upon the current
Of the hazy æther, free
To stretch, in careless strength,
Divinely fashioned wings then
Landing on the branches of a welcoming tree
To fold them neatly
Settle and survey his wondrous element, the sky

But prison bars press hard
Upon his body. No room to even
Open his poor wings – so all day
Long he sings and hops and clings
To each constricting
Bar, hoping
That one will break and let him out into the vibrant world

But nothing moves
Except dull washing
Flapping in the back yard of his prison
And the soaring sound waves of his terrible,
                                        mourning song.

The Last Rites

No, so sorry. I'm entertaining this weekend.
Would love to come, but can't.
I've guests on Monday, I'm afraid.
No, also then – I just can't disappoint.
I know, I'm always busy. Such a
Multitude of friends.

No one had ever been inside
The house – its only occupant
An elderly lady, polite but most remote.
No one had ever seen
One visitor approach that
Large, forbidding door.

When finally they had to
Open it by force,
They stopped, amazed, upon
The threshold of the drawing room,
For there beside her body
Were three cats arranged
As if in prayer
And at the windows birds and
Squirrels chorusing
A strange and dirge-like song

And all around, lit
By dying flames,
Were books, well-read and annotated,
Drawings, papers, poems – her 'friends'
They thought – how sad.

But, as they bent to lift
Her lifeless body, a loud
Lament rose up upon the air,
The cats arched high and hissed,
The windows opened wide
And they stood back in awe
As, silently, the birds and animals
Ranged ceremoniously round her fragile form.

They waited
And the blessèd silence sang.
Then gradually, a warm, unearthly light
Grew up around the mourners and the mourned
Embracing them,
Caressing them
As one.
And then the hallowed creatures sang their last farewell
And took her spirit gently to themselves.

                    And there was peace

                              and then they
Understood. She had not been
A lonely, old eccentric
But a loved and centred lover of all animals and
Birds and
All that is transcendent in mankind.

Morning walk in an October garden

Yes, the web's still there strung between known leaves
The silent spider poisedly centred in his creation;
The robin is still there, hidden, singing quietly in the bushes
Now suprising me by landing like a parachutist
Near my feet.

The dew is there sparkling on each blade of grass
And the yellowing leaf still dangles
On an unseen thread, twirling in an unfelt breeze.

The crows still hold their parliament
And magpies argue with the jays
While, silently, the magnificent crane
Glides, like a dream of Leonardo's, overhead.

Yes, nothing's changed, it seems, but
                    the invisible, inexorable hand of Time.

November View from a Window

Iridescent against the sun-shot darkening sky
A company of seagulls sparkles by
And trees, autumnal in this dallying warmth,
Stand gold and green, still leafy shelters
For the magpie, wren and dove.

But soon, they know, their glory will be stripped
By winds and biting cold, revealing their old
Firm structures, wonderful branching shapes
Of Winter, still offering peace and rest to
Birds and squirrels, a home between the sky and earth.

Let's light the fire and talk of oft-told family tales,
Draw the curtains on our little world, while
Outside, and far beyond our knowing, the trees
Relate their history to the surrounding gods.

Dream of Africa

to Henry Wadsworth Longfellow,
author of The Slave's Dream

Sleeping, he woke in Africa
Beside the lake,
Its healing waters lapping
At his feet,
His Queen and children with him,
The sounds and scents of his
Great kingdom stretching far
Around.
So he was home at last – his
Terrible journey over. A thrilling
Strength surged through his
Noble body. The King had now returned.

Then suddenly
His spine was struck with scorching pain
And he roared out
Enraged. A primitive
Howl roared back, far
Worse than any jungle cry
And he was caught again, in man's horrific trap,
The glaring lights, the ugly sounds, the terrible
Searing pain.
He roared again, a soul in agony,
And mocking echoes and cruel welts
                              fell round him.

He slackened, weakened, gave up his
Dream of Africa, his lioness and cubs
And waited for the iron bars to
Shut him in
To solitary confinement.

View

It is on an early January morning
When birds are praising the new born day
Which most would think as dreary –
                dark etchings of trees against a
                        watercolour sky
          cold and still –
That one can get a sudden glimpse
Of what the world was like
Before the dreadful evolution of mankind.

Air so palpable that birds would
                      seem to swim in it
Water clear and sky-like
                    full of refracting lights
Dappling the glorious travellers of the deep,
Calls and sudden shrieks echoing across the vastness
Rustlings and swishings
Rain pattering lightly on the luscious leaves
Or crashing through the undergrowth
                   like another, giant animal
And overall the peace, the primæval, deep
               unquestioning peace.

Suddenly, unbidden, one senses this lost world –

       in Africa, standing by a pool together with my
                       father
       two humans so out of place and awkward
       in that noble, knowing land stretching to eternity
       whose vast silence is broken only by a
       hippopotamus's yawn and click of
       teeth as slowly, very slowly, he rolls over
                in that unfathomable water

nd here in England on a grey January
awning –   an enfolding, ancient, woodland peace so understood
and praised by animals and birds
o unregarded by this rhythmless, destructive species, man.

Lament and Vision of the Innocent Horse

I weep here in my stall for all my kind.
And particularly, now, for that poor hunted, torn-up fox
        and my poor horse friends, gentle herbivores,
        all forced, with me, by heavy humans,
        to aid and witness his foul murder
                        in the woods.

Those very woods where I, an innocent lilting creature,
Ran exultantly at one with all that lived
(Until man came and broke me).
I knew that fox then as a prancing cub;
He tumbled with his brothers round my feet
        while his dear mother watched us
        trusting in our young companionship.

The very scent of those kind leafy woods
        seeped deep into my flesh then
        so that it seemed I was the wood
            her trees and ferns
            her dappled sunshine
            her creatures and shy flowers.

And yesterday
The instant that I recognised my playfriend, surrounded by mad,
                          ugly murderers,
        that same wood-scent
        seeped through my skin again
        and brought back days of freedom
        joy and bounding strength.

And so I tried to throw my cruel burden, spit out the iron
  from my mouth, run to him through the ravening dogs
  but my natural strength was broken long ago
  – the heavy harness only bit in deeper to
    my clamped and chastised body;

 and weeping as I watched my playfriend
    struggle for his life, both caught by man,
    I tried to send a
    message of pure love and hope
    of higher things beyond this
    soulless world of humans; and as he died
    his eyes met mine in lightning, grateful recognition
        and suddenly
    the whole wild wood lit up
    and there between us
    flared an incandescent flame
    in which I saw his
    spirit rise beyond the baying horde
    and up
    towards a woody, kindly home unknown
        to man
    where rise the spirits of all
      tortured, hunted creatures
      from this sad earth they once called
        mother.

Seaside

And perhaps this is all the baffled human species wants,
To come against eternity in a homely form;
Cricket on the sand, sea soon to wash away their pitch
But not the glory, amazing junior batsmen
And heroic white-haired bowlers relating over tea
Great tales of victory,
Children, now in their own and utterly comprehended element –
Navigators, architects of castles, tellers of ancient tales of
                                        mystery,
Inventors of new games
Marked out with tarns of pebbles, winding channels in the sand
                                        and shells,
Little bucket-carriers crying out to sisters,
'We need more water!', while the sea is huge behind them,
Unlikely people, gratefully stripped now of the corseted
Roles they have to fill, playing quoits with
All the concentration and enjoyment of grand masters,
Elderly couples walking leisurely along the
Clean and level sands, sporting panamas and elegant sunhats,
A picture of Edwardian England,
Two lovers being carefully photographed against
Their own magnificent sand-fort
                                        radiant as the shimmering sun,
Laughter mingling with the cries of seagulls
While the softly swishing sea sings lulling wavesongs
To these now innocent humans.

Wonder

Felix is dreaming of the willow tree.
Last evening, as the wind arose,
He lay beneath its streaming branches
Staring up into its greeny vaults

And as the wind caught one and then another
Weeping strand, he played with it as with
                                             a friend,
His feline eyes the colour of the leaves,
His flowing grace an echo of the tree's.

And I, a poor observer of this mystery,
Stand yet again, unlike the master cat,
A novice on the threshold of philosophy
Which, for us both, begins with wonder.

In Terra Aliena

The Meeting

They came in through the open door
My brother at the front,

So – he was back at last
His death a myth
And all this life a dream.
Same casual aristocratic air,
Familiar jacket, intelligent, blue, musing eyes –
We were together in the family home again
And all my tortured life a dream.

Seeming to wake from nightmare
Into sweet reality
I stretched my arms in welcome
But as I moved
        I heard a door close

Helpless, I woke up into glaring day
While he and the two others his form
                had hidden from sight
Receded into night.

The Arts Club

to J. D. Salinger

Ah! India! Have a drink!
Meet Paul, a poet.
Wonderful! At last, a refuge and a home;
Admired and wanted, brought into the circle.
The surging tears beneath the skin
Cried out to be released
But I held back behind my carefully wrought façade
For fear of spilling all my life
And asked the poet what he thought of
Herbert – the Polish not the English.

I don't <u>read</u> poetry, he said and looked superior.
No way. I write my own.
Oh, I said and smiled,
Politely, feeling small.
We're down here now for good,
His woman said, who wore a hat.
Escaped the rat race
Was in the pantomime.
She smiled a quick and rodent smile and swigged deliberately.

Perched on a proffered bar stool,
Festooned in other people's smoke and noise,
I'd hoped, in my new outfit,
To escape myself, my family and my fears
And meet some nearly-kindred souls.

To drink a glass of wine, or two
Or three
And talk of poetry and loss
Can give a mighty lift
To one whose thoughts have turned to hell.

I've just read Salinger, I said.
A pause.
You've heard of him?
The men around me scoffed and eyed me up and down.
A product of his time.
And I was out of date, though curving where I should
And still a catch.
But have you read him *now*?
The pseuds are still around, I said.
A pause.
And Holden's pain is mine.
Does anybody know, the poet said, accepting yet another drink,
A guy – Siegfried Sassoon – they reckon he's good.
Can't get his books though. In the shops. No way.

The smoke, the drink, the utter loneliness
Gripped like a band around my heart.
Travel nine or ninety miles, you'll
Always meet with this – the same dull-lit and smoky hell
You thought was home,
Just you are different
Like Holden and his old museum pieces.

Surely, I said, with all the
First World War commemorations, there must be lots of stuff
                                                    around.

I felt more confident again.
Was it the wine
Or my home ground of loss and searing sensibility
Or both?

What incredible loss there was, I said; yes
There is Sassoon;
But Wilfred Owen –
That most moving poem
Which begins . . .

Not heard of `im, the poet said.

Isolation

Solidified by loneliness,
He turns a rock-hewn face
Towards the world
Which, judging at face-value,
Passes by

And
Leaves him stranded
On the opposite shore
Of that fast, icy river
Which flows between the members of mankind.

     His only choice to swim
          or sink into oblivion.

Alien

One day, I'm going to leave the
Train at Vauxhall, cross the road
To that most innocent building
I have gazed upon so often,
Enter the portals of the
British Interplanetary Society
And ask for help.

I came here by mistake,
I'll say. I can't remember – but
I must have fallen,
Lost my way in space,
Taken the wrong turning – but for whatever
                reason I now find myself on Earth
                I cannot settle
                cannot understand men's rules and way of death
                cannot understand their hatred of all life,
                their constant planning for destruction,
                their lack of song and dance and rhythm,
                and, most of all, their total lack of joy.

Sometimes, alone, the wind has whispered
That he'll take me back and I have leapt and tried to
                        sail with him
But always fallen.

The birds, as well, have sung to me
Thinking they'll soothe me with remembrance.
But it only makes it worse.

Trees also make me weep. I look at those great
Friends and see the chainsaw's shadow.

It's no use, I'll say. I've tried,
I've tried to naturalise – but
                    how can I?
Apart from shuddering aversion to being member
                of a cruel race
There is the problem of communication.

My language is not known here –
I've tried, I really have, with varied
Cadence, intonation, pausing, breath,
Tone colour. And then silence – and
This once or twice has worked – a
Spark has gleamed and flickered in the dark.
But that is all.
And I am lonely
Oh, so lonely
In this terrible place.

This is what I'll say to them
In that large room I sometimes see at dusk
                    with the glowing chandelier.

And perhaps they'll welcome me.
          Perhaps they'll have
          A Missing List, there, in the hall
          And on it I will read my name
          And under will be written
          'If she reports to you, please give
          Indemnity of passage.'

And in the clubroom of the British Interplanetary Society
I'll sink into an armchair
And drink a farewell toast to this
Sad, beautiful planet men call Earth.

New lamps for old! New lamps for old!

sapere aude.
Horace, Epistles 1 ii 40

Do not surrender your old lamp,
The dull, unburnished and old-fashioned one –
In the attic perhaps? or a cupboard? –
Almost forgotten, but, for some reason
Never thrown out.

Do not listen to the clangorous voice
Offering a brassy, empty substitute
(For your life – for your real life.)

For it is all there – all your treasured
Glimpses of eternity – loves – all there
In that old-fashioned vessel
Which somehow just doesn't fit
In – would be
A bit of an embarrassment in
Drawing room or even kitchen
   – an odd and unexplainable artefact
(And one has to try and live in society).

Yet someone has caught scent of it
Someone wants it – is offering
A brand new lamp for it.

        (And yet what he has failed to realise
        Is that when he calls out the genie
        It will not be at home – all he will
        Conjure up will be black, ugly smoke.)

No, treasure your old lamp –
Bring it out beside the fire,
Forgetting what the flimsy world denotes
                              as 'right'.
Have the courage to be wise
Expand into your element
Bring in the sea and sky and air
And gently, very gently, burnish
                    the lamp into a
Shining vessel – and then

          As Time renounces his proud sway
          And the material world vanishes
          And what is real gradually becomes manifest
          All those seemingly lost moments
                    will pour forth as from a cornucopia
                              of revelation.

The Dinner Party

Last night, I had a dinner party
With Wilfred Owen, Harold Monro
And Borges.

We drank wine, laughed, forgot to eat
And, of course, wept freely.
I told them how I loved their work
How long-ago I used to recite, 'The wind feels hard enough
                                   to-night
To crack the stars, and bring them down;'
On my way to my Saturday morning speech and drama class,
Learning it as I walked, how Owen's, 'Move him into the sun – '
Had always moved me and how the truthfulness
Of Borges gave me hope in this untruthful time.

We stayed up late, musing and reading, reciting
And drinking and finally it was I who was tired –
They were ready to go on till morning and beyond –
But I was heady and drowsy with their terrible beauty.
And then, as we parted, they said, 'And
You, too, are one of us. We know. We understand.'

The Lucie Darling School of Poetry Modelling

1) Hi-Kew

dress: kimonos
make-up: white base
black eye-liner
defined red lips

`oday we will learn how to write Hi-Kew.
`hink of an object – anything, a flask of perfume
`n electric toaster – write it down. Then think of
`ome short whimsical lines, preferably unconnected with your object.
`Vrite it down, with naice spaicing, and there
`s your Hi-Kew. For example,

Chanel Number Five
The wind rising in the North
Will he bring me a flacon?

`nd, en passant, darlings, please forget those dubious
`oreign Japanese origins - absolutely non-U for Hi-Kew
and not in English either!

`ext week we will have a competition
`udged by the actor, poet, writer, publisher, international model
`nd popular TV Personality, Horatio Spineless.
`Vhoever cen recite the greatest number of their
`wn unpublished and unexpurgated Hi-Kew
`1 Two Minutes – and Remember my ruthless, ringing stop-watch -
`Vill be the winner and
`ublished on our own Lucie Darling Website, Jingles.
`lso, and please wear the correct outfit for this,
`Refer to your outfit list) and darlings, you all
`ook divine today in your kimonos, we will learn the quick,
`ail-safe method of Sonnet writing. And remember darlings –
`aice posture, head high, step out confidently, from the hips, for
`hose who write Hi-Kew all have high I.Q.!

2) Sonnets

dress: Elizabethan
girls: pronounced cleavage
      (Wonderbra I wonder?)
boys: tights and codpiece
      (and no tittering)
make-up: pink and white
      patches for the girls

a	If, then, my loving you is cause of	**hurt**
b	I'll straight refuse all wholesome food and	**drink**
a	And never with the lovely maidens	**flirt**
b	But into dreadful apathy will	**sink.**
c	I'll lie upon my silken bed	**alone**
d	And shade the glaring lights with softest	**cloud,**
c	Faint Musick shall becalm my saddest	**moan**
d	While I eschew all daring ventures	**loud.**
e	Considering men's company but	**vile**
f	And every wench's gleaming bosom	**cold,**
e	I'll never with my lips your name	**defile**
f	Or think your precious trinkets ought but	**gold.**
g	And if you now within my chamber	**stood**
g	I'd promise on my knee that I'd be	**good.**

Today, darlings, and what cod-pieces, Berman's are a joy!,
I am handing out the fail-safe plan of sonnet modelling.
Stage One - write out the rhyme scheme, as easy as ABC, Darlings,
See your left-hand column. There are three options – the other two
On reverse of your sheet. Next, darlings, no don't
Put your handkerchief there, Jocasta, it will spoil the shape,
Write any correctly rhyming words you like in the
Right hand column, as I have – then just fill in the space in-between.

took just five minutes to fill mine in – Yes, Donald
asier than a census form!
What did I tell you last week you lovely darlings,
asy-peesy. Now run away – don't mince, GLIDE, yes, even if
                                      they are tight!
And sonneteer like mad, because the Principal,
Pevensey Piecemeal, will want to hear all, and I mean all,
your divine sonnets. And remember darlings,
Back again, oh we do work hard, don't we,
in ten minutes, for the Hi-Kew Competition with Horatio.
And next week it's The Lyric – again correct costume, please!
And remember, Sonneteers to all are dear! Especially Lucie Darling's!

3) The Lyric

dress: girls: Shepherdess costume
                     looped-up petticoats
                     same cleavage as 'Sonnets'
                     ribbons in hair
        boys: Shepherd's costume
props: lyre; pan pipes

Today, I want to teach you some difficult words
That will help you immensely with your Lyric work –
Swain, haycock, lass, trill, Pan, linger.
'Swain' means a young, lower class or peasant
Worker who thinks he's in love; 'haycock', no it
Is not a rough form of greeting, Donald, is
A stack of hay left in a field for collection, under which
                                peasants sat.
'Lass' is a peasant or lower-class, country girl.
'Trill' is what birds do and peasants do on pipes.
'Pan' is a sort of god with goat's legs. No nothing
To do with the Church of England, Julian. 'Linger'
Means what we mustn't do, stand about not
Getting anywhere. Now, imagine you are
Sitting in a field under a 'haycock', either
'Trilling' on a pipe or hearing one in the distance.
You are in love with a 'lass', who works on
The next farm over the hill. Now write something
Very flowing like the girls' ribbons. Yes, I know it
Is difficult to imagine how the working-class think
(If, indeed, they do). But this is poetry - just make it
Simple and a bit soft. For example, here is a first quick
Stanza: *My lass, she lives o'er yonder hill.*
                I fain would know if ought is ill.

I wait today all in the sun
And not to me is my love come.
This haycock is but a crude bed,
For one who will, by Hymen led,
Lie with her 'neath the glowing sky
While Pan trills us a lullaby.

You can forget for the moment the classical reference,
No it is not an anatomical name, Jocasta, (not here, anyway)
I just needed something for the rhyme scheme.
Now all you sweet shepherds and shepherdesses
Linger awhile, while I go and talk to Pevensey
In the Blue Room, and write me some wonderful lyrics.
Just waft like fleecy clouds around the room and it will come
                                                    to you
And remember, Lyrical Verse puts money in the purse!

Street Chat
or
the unimportance of events

Fantastic! A non-stop
whirl Disneyland Nightclubs
Colarado Rockies great food
non-stop coffee drive-in movies
Fifth Avenue I bought some really
silly shoes shocking pink and
shocking price but really USA
I mean you've got to go before
the kids grow up they need
the rich experience to say they've
been there all their friends have
popcorn like you've never had before
but that's enough of me how're you
done anything been anywhere.

Not really. I've been reading.

Anything special.

Eliot, George and T.S.,
Wells and Hardy, Thomas, R.S.,
Dylan and the Edward and
Some Shakespeare, mainly *Hamlet*.

Any good? You look exhausted.

They're not relaxing people.

Get out. Do something
really cheap flights now

you'd love Disneyland
books are OK on shelves and stacked
away in libraries – but they're not
Life. Just look at what
we've done in just two weeks
while you've been stuck indoors
the places we have seen.
Get Out is my advice before the cobwebs get you.

I'll definitely think about it.
They waved goodbye and parted,
One into her TV guarded house,
Which kept the family safely grounded by a screen,
The other to her unsafe library
And secret magic carpet
Which flew her far beyond the reach
Of plane or nosing camera
And left her æons later
Exhausted with no souvenirs to speak of
Save a tiny jewelled map
Of strange contoùr
And wildly haunting music
Whirling through her veins.

Hölderlin's Retreat into Darkness

No, not for long can one endure the piercing shaft
The sudden searing through the body of lightning recognition
The leap to meet the all-consuming flame.

Not for long can one remain, like Socrates, a smiling citizen of the
world
Polite and conscientious, paying taxes, teaching
Whilst suddenly, at any time, this
Dreadful agony darts through one, beaming strange, penetrating light
Upon the glowing vision
As though one stood upon a magic pinnacle
And saw the All spread out in contour,
Saw suddenly Dionysus, Christ and Buddha, Empedocles
Calling for kind peace, cessation of blood-shed, saw all Divines
All Lovers, Hero and Leander and the shrouding Hellespont
Cleopatra clasping death to her wild, mourning breast,
Saw wondrous Nature in Her unity, the soaring tree and busy ant
The yawning crocodile and caring ape, divine winged creatures,
The holy water-dwellers, all haloed in embracing Æther,
Saw again one's childhood vision of the splendour in the grass,
While far below in stinking caves the greedy creeping cruelty of man
Tries desperately to destroy it.

Not long can one stand on the threshold of Eternity
Conducting holy fire.
Something will break.

Frightened jealous fools will offer hemlock, murderous assault,
a cross.
Drunkeness or madness will draw down the blind
Leaving the poet distanced,
Smiling at visitors to his quiet abode
Smiling beyond their prying, stupid stares

miling towards a terrible, aching void
                              that is his own
Vhilst in the untenanted hall of his great mind
oft shadows murmur ceaselessly.

The Ghost

Like a ghost who cannot grasp that Time is real
She haunts the places where she once was young.

There! No, there! Beside the family tree
The crossroads in the background and
The ever-gliding river in our view,
The noble silhouette of Hampton Court
Darkening to a sketch as
The burnished water flames
Towards the falling sun and wheeling birds
Trace elegant patterns in the sky.
Yes, here I feel at home.

But even as the thought warms in her soul
Night comes; and ugly voices, sounds so unfamiliar,
Shatter the delicate vision; and she stands,
Once more alone, a ghost
Without a home.

The Clearing in the Forest

When you come upon a clearing
In the Forest of Despair,
Note it down with care.

Note the quality of light,
The luminous essence of each form,
The secret web between them drawn.

Note the lack of temporal sway,
The strange clarity of air,
Note it down with loving care.

Think that others also come
To this green, secret glade
And rest their dreadful wounds in healing shade.

This is the place that
Hölderlin has seen, Clare,
Schubert, Shelley, all have been bright visitors.

This is Reality, this timeless place,
The Truth beyond the terrible façades,
The Golden City with its honest guards.

O, remember, try to remember, O, dear friend,
The Clearing in the Forest with its healing air
When you again become benighted by despair.

Other Dimensions

Übergang

On the edge of waking from a dream
Where the fragmented soul hovers,
Like a haze of dancing insects in the waning dusk,
Before re-entering another plane

Vistas of lives beckon;
So temptingly that only, it seems, the inability to decide
Which path prevents the soul's return.

There, is the familiar wall, patchy with moss and lichen,
Webbed tiny holes and red valerian, the sunlight mellow
And the lane inviting in its quiet, afternoon warmth;
There is the darkening street in Holland Park, the
Noble house, the awning ready to receive
Its guests, myself among them, into its lit, welcoming
Hall and then the glittering ballroom where he, I know, awaits.

And there is the dark, college corridor,
Familiar but unknown
The discipline exacting
Leading me into further corridors of the mind
                         and further planes of being.

And there and there and there, are paths of possibilities
                         now fading on the day
While, here, the hovering soul gathers and returns
Bringing the dreamer
Into yet another difficult birth.

Falling into further dreaming of being

Glad that the troublesome night is over,
My dreams reluctantly retreating to their dark abode,
I contemplate the day

Yet they will not go away and chase the daylight
With their strange configurations, I a mere
Conductor of their vibrant life;

For this silent strife confuses all my actions
Colours my responses, so that I seem to dream anew
Or they dream me into the daily light

And my very sight is altered. Trees move, gleaming strangely
And the sky and visionary cloud-banks beckon,
Inviting me into a world of shimmering beauty

So straightway I am hurled into a further dream of being
Where past and present lose all meaning,
All that is, is real, the illusory day retreats and I am home at
last.

Dreaming of relating a dream

It was Waterloo station
My father was buying tickets
At an old-fashioned ticket office next to Platform 1
I had just heard that the attack
Was to be in six or seven days' time
The final world-obliterating attack

I woke up, terrified,
Would it include Paris?
I tried to be normal calling
To my father as I joined
My mother walking towards the
Exit, not to forget *The Times* –
There was a good Arts page, I said, he picked one off a stand
Began reading from it aloud – no one I
Knew – tedious hackneyed phrases

We reached the main
Exit and began descending the once
Grand steps – now worn away
Just earth and tufts of dirty grass
The handrails rotten.

Where were we going? Nowhere
That required railway tickets
Why had he purchased them
The end of the world

The end of the known world

Ex Stasis

Faintly aware of sounds I should respond to
I slowly surfaced up through shores of singing silence,
Observing, as I did, the heavy weight of limbs
(Had Lilliputians tied me to the bed?)
Together with a strangely soaring warmth and lightness in my
                                                            body.

I felt like Alice flying backwards up the rabbit hole,
Noting, instead of jars, the topoi
Of my dream – a boat, a stretch of
Water, a house wherein
A woman whirled upon a
Roulette board, spreadeagled, people kneeling.

I wanted to escape and took a train
Which showed me on its route the
Lives of other people lit up flatly
In their peepshow houses.
But the shows were all the same – commonplace and small,
The TV, roulette table and the kneeling horde.

The train drew to a halt.
I had returned to where I started from
But this was not a fugal resolution, no Eliot recognition,
No circling Miðgarðsorm to keep me warm.
It spelt despair.
The depravity of normality loomed hugely round me like a trap.

I sank into the gulf
But could not drown, so climbed some iron steps
Onto the boat
Only to meet the people from
The house in evening dress
Descending from a party – long burnt out.

Heavily I climbed up one more step
Onto the empty deck.
In desolation, I kicked the dirty stubs and shrivelled party mess.
I kicked again and felt the Lilliputian bonds release.

Slowly the needle points receded
Leaving me
Stunned upon the bed
Awake.

Sounds I should attend to!
Another day.
Another day to face.

First find the mask.

Which shall it be? Comedy?

Doppelgänger

Was it a dream or actuality
That as I walked down Church Road
To catch the bus to school
(that innocent bus which, when told off
for lateness, my friend and I
explained away as having merged into
the background – so that in fact, we seriously said,
to the mistress's extreme chagrin,
we had not really missed the bus because
the bus had not been really there),
I saw myself standing
In the doorway of a house
So real, it's with me still
That strange, familiar recognition of my self apart from me?

Often I see her there,
Vibrant in the midst of present life,
Shy, lithe body,
School uniform neat but somehow separate,
Apprehensive angle of the head,
Standing, hesitant, upon the threshold
Of an unknown house
Seeming dazzled by the morning sun.

Which of us moved forward then
To take the deadly route to school,
The bus, the jostling, the dash into
The classroom, reluctantly shrugging on
The role of silly, giggling pupil
But really desperate for the *richtige Nahrung*
Like Kafka's Gregor,
She or I?

Which of us has always
Missed the obvious bus
Because it merged into the background
Of our more real thoughts?

Which of us, in fact, is real?
Or are we
Each a figment of the
Other's mind?
Did she see me, I wonder,
Walking down the dreary road to school
And does she now remember me
In sudden moments when she isn't thinking
And unbidden, strange unwonted images flit into her mind
Like pterodactyls flying into fairyland?

Which one is real?
Or, echoing the Priest Saigyō,

If reality is not real
And dreams are then not dreams,
Do we both exist
Beyond the confines of the real and dream?

And if we do, shall we then meet one day
Beyond this heavy time
And fall into each other's arms and cry,
I tried but did not have the means
And wherewithal to live this earthly life,

I really could not see the buses and the
Obvious goals.

Most times I lived as in a spell,
The gossamer shine of beauty
Competing with Mephisto-like negation
For possession of my soul.

Having once seen the living grass,
The bird alight upon the singing tree,
The fern unfurling,
The moon half-hidden in a watery haze,
How can one live amongst the TV and the news?
How can one weakly witness
The sad destruction of this cobweb life
Which is the only strength we have?

Shall we talk thus,
Shall we be sister souls
And shall we find a way to
Live before we die?

Station Café
or
The Immortality of Dreams

'You want to stop 'ere,' she said.
'Better'n Lincoln King John
Died 'ere
Museum t'river casstle – mooch better!'

The languid woman with obnoxious child
To whom this exhortation was addressed,
Heard the approaching train and gathering busy bags
Bestowed, by way of answer,
Just one tight smile upon the
Garrulous dispenser of refreshments.

'Well stop off on t'weay back
He we'er a reight lad 'ere King John,' she said,
'All soarts of escapades.'

The train came in and, noisily important, they banged
Out from the little twinkling-windowed café
To the chill February fairy-story station
                    (which held no magic for their eyes)
Displaying that supreme indifference to all around them
That only quick-rich Southerners can acheive, and
Leaving me, sole occupant, trying to ignore the notices
Which read, THIS IS NOT A WAITING ROOM. CUSTOMERS
                                                    ONLY.

'Wea've got t'Magna Carter 'ere!' she called
                in warm and unoffended tones, a last enticement.

I also had to get the train and turned
To see this fervent courtier of King John,
Beholding, with first common view, a heavy
Ageing woman in dull, shapeless clothes
And bunion out-pressed shoes polishing
With loving care a winking counter, bearing paper cups and
                                                      cakes.

        but, as I left,
                  I saw her lithely bend beneath it
                  Blushingly - eyes shining
                  To check the casks once more
And buff the evergleaming, golden goblet chased with silver
Ready for King John when he should
Rampage through her glittering café
                         and call for
        Escapades
            for wine
                and song
                    and her!

Magic

to J. B. P.

Yes, it is the touch of magic
That transforms the world. The hint
Of vibrant life beyond
This bartered earth, the fairy wing
Just glimpsed through slanting rain
Spheres singing
Through the human din.

It is the lost Atlantis of the mind
That cancels out as void
The niggardly, dull ledgers of enjoyment
Fussily bound in dusty board
And chronologically stacked in airless cellars.

It is the flash of vision
That gives hope
Transforming this poor world
Into a paradise garden where, through the
Flowery arch, one sees the gleaming steps to heaven.

MOTHER - 1918

in memory of my great-grandmother
Mary Ann Russell *née* Fish

In the darkest of dread London nights came the
Long awaited sound.
She breathed, once more alive,
'Albert! Back!'
Love and relief flooded through her so long
                                    pent-up body
As she heard him climb the stairs
And call out 'Mother!'

'Albert's come home! He's safe!', she
Cried to her still sleep-caught husband.
The relief! The blessèd blest relief.
Weeping with joy, she rushed to meet him,
Her prayers at last were answered.

But it was not he.
The stairs were empty. The door still locked. Black rain
                        still falling on blank eyeless streets.

When the telegram came,
They read that he had died upon the very instant
She had heard him call to her.
He died bravely and with honour, wrote the field-nurse,
And, she added in soft, understanding pencil,
His dying word was, 'Mother!'.

Leaving the Flowers

Slowly the unordered pattern appears.
For years she's lived with
Death
     her son, killed suddenly,
News crashing like a dinosaur
Through the garden of our lives.

And now, she too departs,
Leaving the flowers.

     Birds wheel across the sky
     And Autumn leaves fall
     Past my eyes like jewelled tears.
     The undertakers doff their hats
     And bow like puppets
     To my mother's coffin
     And my self begins to crack.

     The ground rears up
     Like everlasting ice
     But a friend's voice
     Pulls me back,
     'Oh, Margaret.'

     I must stand up
     Although I want to join the wheeling birds
     And fly at desperate angles to the earth. I
     Want to climb up to the sky and
     Soar beyond the limits of mere
     Birth and death.
     I want to soar and scream
     And be a seagull.

But I walk obediently and straight and
Ground my aching soul into my hands.

But when I stand and say
The Eliot verse, beginning
     'Home is where one starts from.',
I feel again my soul begin to
Rise and fly
And, fearing that I'll spoil the ordered pattern,
I force myself to ground and shout
Out to the congregation, like a sergeant major,
'In my end is my beginning.'!

And then it's over
And we go,
Leaving the flowers.

Now, after the event,
The smiling Prebendary,
The gospel and the shrouded end,
The tears and sleepless nights,
The utter desolation in this raucous, fair-ground world,
I suddenly remember
Chekhov, like a friend.

He, too, was kind and gentle
Like my mother,
Listening to music beyond the human blare,   •
He too respected life
Allowing others pause and space to grow
And found untimely death through selfless ministration

And I am pleased
That his same image
Has visited me, with its
Releasing wings

He, too, left gentle spaces
And kind silences
And flowers.

The Lovers

Like cast-off shells, no longer relevant,
The bodies of the lovers lie discarded by the ocean
While far below they know
The throbbing moan of birth and death
That issues from the surface of the earth,
Pushing the waves and ripples of the
Swelling seas through veins and arteries
And trees and leaves and crashing stars.

Ridden over by sea horses and whispered to
By smiling fish, they lie upon that ancient bed
Reluctant to return to terrible separateness,
Reluctant to know again by brain what now they
                                            know by
Watery sense – the vehement, explosive
                              nature of all being

The Apex

You say you don't remember
That all-important conversation
There in leafy Malet Street;
The wise and ancient spirits
Drifting from the great Museum and
Mingling with the modern Godless Ones of Gower Street,
My father and myself amongst them.

I remember how it changed my life,
Weaving it inextricably with yours.
I remember the witnessing elegant house, the
Noble trees, the sunken garden and the shadowy
Iron railings

I remember
The sudden, brilliant flare of love
As frightening and reassuring as
Those giant, daring souls
Sailing beyond the known and charted skies.

The Reading Room

It was a Music of the Spirit that arose
Echoing round the sounding Dome and on
Beyond the known and breathing air to
Temples of Athene and Poseidon,
And on, to the great pyramids of the Pharaohs,
Then circling to the listening stars who sang
Again for joy to know
There were still ears could hear the Music of the Spheres,
Still souls fostering the growth of
Truth and Beauty

And like two meeting tides
Rising in ecstasy of recognition,
The heavenly music sang out
Returning divine vibrations
Down the man-made centuries
Until Time vanished and pure Thought
Embraced by Soul stood shimmering
In the new and timeless Moment and
Surrounded all earnest Students of Philosophy,
There in the quiet
Radiating Reading Room in Bloomsbury
High above the bustle of the time-bound
Day – a visible temple
              of invisible thought
A sanctuary;

              which like so many holy places
Now lies desecrated by the jealous heathens and
Open to the mindless eyes of tourists
              and the chipped and clockwork world.

Finale

Piano Sonata in B flat D960

The pianist waits, and the coughers and shufflers
                         attempt some attention;
The walls of the concert hall waver and melt;
The clocks stop;
The air becomes thin;
And the spirit of Schubert forks down
                              like lightning
Onto the keys
Piercing
With the terrible surgeon's simple skill
The tragic well-springs of our ills.

And those who hear through not
                         with the ear
Must ascend again the lonely crag of the heart
Must again suffer themselves to be opened up
                stripped of flesh
                exposed to the passion of those
                lacerating airs
'hile far below, on the sunny uplands, the peasants dance.

It cannot be borne but the notes move on
                and the G octave is relentless
                            driven;

And then it's over
           the whole operation
           veins burning
           through scourged bodies, eyes blinded;

And the coughers and shufflers are clapping like mad
While time trips over itself thinking of dinner
And a hideous bouquet is being presented
To Schubert's pale messenger
And the sponsors are counting their gains.

The Invitation

When dryads no longer dance
And fauns are frighted from the unshadowy Earth
And the pall of the Second Enlightenment
Stifles the spirit
Turn
And turn again into the mind,
Climb the spiral stairs into its
Turrets and there
             look out into the vasty sky.

The wind blows cold and loneliness
Will grip you in its terrible embrace
But wait and listen

Endure

Faintly but reassuringly the music of the spheres
Sends its unworldly strains and gradually
Faint shapes, recalling dreams and friends,
Form into majestic patterns – patterns
You had always known and seen – in seashells
Animals and sighing trees, patterns you had sensed
In daily life
         the intonation of a voice
         the trembling of a leaf
         the calling of your name by loved ones, long ago

Take heart now

As loneliness falls from you like a cloak
The sky shifts
Heavenly forests spread out

And Syrinx is heard

Turn
    just once more

                The dryads are dancing again
         And beautiful fauns, shade-dappled,
         Invite you, calling your name, into celestial groves.

The Transformation

And as she woke she felt
Long tresses of green tracery
Arching above and round her
A shelter in which to grow
And regain strength. Her body
Pulsed with strange and urgent energy
And she no longer felt afraid of
The peculiar world of humans for
Her thoughts were now transmuted into
Singing feeling and she knew she
Was no longer of their kind. And
As the insubstantial trappings of her
Former life fell back into a mist
She rose up weeping
And was a willow.

The Kaleidoscope of Time

First Valentine

You were the sun that glanced in my hair
You were the fun with never a care

You were the fern, the mouse and the hill
You were the house for which I yearn still.

You were the harbour which sheltered my tears
You were the arbour which charmed away fears

You were the earth on which I skipped high
You were the birth of my opening eye.

Ours was the dewdrop upon the first flower
Ours was the future, the day and the hour.

And now many things block my first cloudless view
I languish, remember and dwell upon you

And wish I could turn and return to your gaze
And laugh and find shelter from life's dreadful maze.

Memory Lane

Across the sparkling Thames at busy Waterloo,
Under Monet's Bridge,
Along dark, twisting alleyways
    with sudden gleams of light
    and ghastly shadows,
Under the railway arch
    where the first thrilling kiss still breathes its magic –
        rain on the wind, a rush of urgent passion
        school uniforms too conspicuous,

Along the sepia banks of Rackham's faery river, beneath
                        stark, wintering willows
    towards the beckoning sky;

Through the gate into the Secret Garden,
    the latch just reached on tiptoe,
Under the rustic arch
Blowing with Grandpa's roses,
Down the tangled path
Past frames and flower pots
And smiling, nodding flowers,
    the peonies like secret friends,
And on, beyond the deck chairs, to the gleaming grass
Of childhood where
I find a four-leafed clover
And press it in the Bible
Which I cannot read.

From Teragram to Llessur

One day, do you remember, while we were playing
And exchanging serious confidences,
(We used to leave each other
coded messages at night
under the landing carpet
as if the day weren't long enough for secrets),
We discovered that we both could fly.

My circumstance was quite mundane.
I'd flown downstairs over the top
Of a lot of relatives in the hall
(Uncle John was there) and out through the door
And I'd been worried as I flew
That I might touch them on the
Head and make them jump.
But, as it happened, they didn't notice.

Your story I can't recall,
Or maybe you didn't give any details
Only that you were absolutely
Confident that you could fly,
That it was part of your life.

> And now you are not part of my life,
> Now Death's pall and appalling screen
> Has cut you off for so long,
> I often wonder and think
> Of our power
> And wish we could use it
> To meet somewhere
> And seriously talk
> Of how we both fare.

(I know you're there,
You're my brother.)

But in my dreams
You always elude me
And I wake up crying
And feel like dying.

The Secret High Jumper

After school, on the hushed, summer-warm playing field,
No one at the classroom windows but the occasional
Lone girl, kept in on detention,
I would practise, or rather, exult in,
High Jump.

The run-up, the sudden lift-off from familiar grass
Into the ever-changing, school-free air
Which slowly and securely embraced my sailing body
Was quite magical. If I'd grown wings
I could not have felt more earth-free or released.

And then the gentle landing, seemingly hours after,
When I would quietly, as though not wishing to disturb
Propitious gods, raise the bar
Run back to my soft starting place
And once again begin my wonderful ascent. It was
Intoxicating. God-given. And a Secret.

But then, one day, the striding Games Mistress just happened
To see me. I, who was 'unsporty', 'bright', 'silly'
'Boy-mad' (and, for some reason, a school prefect)
Was now to Represent The School.
And at the first bleak Competition, my god of flight
Deserted me. There, on that loud Athletics Ground
Where tough-limbed, strutting girls in masterful shorts and
spikes
Measured professional paces to the bar
I, who'd never counted but just jumped,
Became uncertain, wavered, copied their proud movements
And was, of course, disqualified.
'Three No-Jumps!' rang across my heat-hazed head.

And grounded in the adult, grey-dimensional world
                              I took the sad bus home.

And often in this heavy time
I suddenly glimpse those far-off, sunny days
And wish, oh wish
I'd never doubted
                    I could fly.

Ø

In a little boat on a transparent, silently-stretching lake,
The watching Norwegian mountains haloed by such
Scintillating air that seeing seemed like vision
Or was vision,
I suddenly saw a towering rock beneath the
Water. 'Oye!' I cried out, frightened.
'Jo, jo!', they replied, smiling.
And I wondered at their strange response.

We rowed on, safely, towards another rock, this time
Above the water, where we moored and scrambled
Over crevices and cracks until
We came upon a flat and sloping plane where
The others built a bonfire. How or where they gathered
Kindling I can't recall, but in those student days
All things seemed possible – even the
Lighting of a Sankt Johannes bål on a bare and
Lake-encircled rock to give
More power to the sun, while we drank
Aquavit on a glowing St. John's morning and
I fell deep in love with a wild, romantic left-wing student
Who sang me haunting, strange Norwegian-Jewish songs
Calling me 'havfruen min' – my mermaid.

And I half-believed him, dreaming of
Our own enchanted island beneath
The water – and then suddenly realised why
They'd smiled when I'd cried 'Oye!'
Remembering that 'ø' meant island.

Perhaps then that would be our secret place
And we could sink beneath the enfolding lake

And stop time
And I could always be his mermaid and comb my
Flowing hair while he sang haunting
Songs of long ago and we
Would never have to move towards this cruel, blaring world
But live together happily, there beneath the hushing, loving water
Happily for ever and ever after.

Es war einmal ...

In those days when innocence and kindness
And the golden haze of fairy tales
Seemed part of the very air one breathed

We all sat in a Gasthof, my parents,
Brother and University friend, the wild grape curling at
The door, the friendly buzz of local conversation,
Ours the only foreign language there, in that
Gemütlich, dark interior, when I said,
Reading an inviting notice, 'There's a Feuermannsfest
This evening – oh, let's go!'

And innocently we climbed the steep
And darkening hill, up and up and up and darkening still,
So remote and quiet that trees and bushes
Seemed like giants in a land beneath the stars,
When, suddenly, the sound of merry fiddling and
The gleam of welcome from a Hütte welcomed us.

And then we realised – it was a private Fest! But magically
We were drawn in and there among them at a table,
Brimming jugs before us, smiling eyes
And the Dudelsack and Geige sang a
Spell-like dance while the whirling figures on the wooden floor,
The fairy tale Dirndls and soft German voices lulled me
In a trance; and as the sturdy firemen
Bowed and asked my mother for this dance and the next
And then the next – I saw her as a
Princess in a story – dancing an
Enchanted dance beneath the stars, safe in the strong arms
Of a Feuermann – so nimble-footed, so beautiful
And so eternally young – and I knew
She could not die.

And as we sat there, my father never dancing,
Amused at her so sudden popularity,
I felt our family in that enchanted Hütte
Inextricably bound and yet each destined
Soon to take a different path.

And as, singing with the singing, tingling stars,
We all went gaily down that night and heady-scented hill,
I felt a deep intolerable sadness
That the magic could not last.

        But now, I wonder – they are all
Gone, but I wonder.

Recognition

My mouth weeping with tears
And my eyes heavy with the sadness of the years
I went into a Chemist's for some painkillers,
Oh, would there were a remedy for pain,
When a travelling salesman suddenly addressed me,
His jolly face alight with recognition,
'You're local aren't you? I've seen you here.'
'In Browns', I said. 'Yes, I knew I
Seen you,' he said, pleased with his perspicacity,
'I'm here every month, with these novelties
They go down well.' He held a large black
Furry spider with bulging eyes, for my inspection.
I laughed and said I didn't want one.
'They go down well 'ere specially at the Hallowe'en
See you next month then'. We waved goodbye like friends.

In Browns. Why had I said that?
In Browns, once, with a boyfriend, how long ago?, an eager
                                        girl then
On a thrilling pilgrimage to Laugharne, where, breathlessly,
I bought two Dylan Thomas books in
Manchester House, faded and forgotten
The bookseller seemingly suprised to see them on his shelves;
An eager, open-spirited girl, ready for life and love
But utterly unprepared for the tragedies that
Waited in her path. Unprepared
For the terrible realities of life
But innocently and familiarly open to the unrealities –
The visions, recognitions, co-incidences
That were not co-incidental, instinctively aware of
The unreality of Time.

You're local aren't you I knew I'd seen you
I'm here every month
In Browns, I said.
That's it! I knew I'd seen you.

The Boundaries of Whidown

The boundaries of Whidown were unknown,
Bushes merging into tangled woods,
Grass walking wildly past the stream into the copse
To join meandering, illimitable paths,
The mossy bridges arching into fairyland,
All vistas of exciting possibilities,
     untrodden pathways of the mind.

And every night, as I flew off within my dreams
And left them sleeping on that lonely hill,
I worried that I might not find our boundless sanctuary again,
Might never more explore with them the curves and mysteries
     of Time, might never see again
     the flash of Paradise,
     the glinting stream,
     the welcome rooves of home.

But it was always there, half floating in the morning mist,
Caught between white scarves of light, the foxes
Coughing in the woods, the buzzards mewing overhead
     like flying cats,
The house becoming solid, imposing its unbounded and enquiring
     dignity on the day.

And now, last night, I dreamt that I was there again,
Walking through the grounds in conversation with my father.
And all around were workmen, industrious, intent,
Ignored by us, putting up fences, close in to the house.
Everywhere. Banging the wooden planks with
     measured care.

Even the hedge-gaps in the paddock and
Beside the lawn that faced the lane were being filled
With dreadful, spiked enclosures.

And I wondered, as I dragged myself
From sleep, why they were putting boundaries
Round Whidown, now we all had left.

The Balloon

It's still there, by the keys,
Disintegrating,
Picked out delicately with tweezers
By the piano tuner,
Bright, ossified fragments of another world.

Who played the piano then, I wonder,
Lid propped open, wineglass
Close to hand – an uncle,
Grandfather or friend,
Cigar smoke wreathing
Round the other decorations;
The laughter, family jokes and fun,
The clink of glasses,
Uncles, great-aunts, parents well-disposed and fed,
Their world complete and circumscribed by paper chains and
hats
And coloured, gay balloons,
While we two children revelled in our other world
embraced by theirs?

The cruel kaleidoscope of time
inevitably shifts, regardless of the pattern that it breaks
And gives no answer
while the old piano stands
Victorianly black and mute,
Bereft of wine glasses
And mirth, bereft of voices redolent
Of love and family solidarity,
Bereft now even of its little
Secret –   the bright balloon which

Long ago, amidst the merriment and fun,
    sailed down into its heart
And which it cradled in a vain
Attempt to keep the party spirit going.

And now its darling, wrested from its all-preserving depths,
Lies turning back to dust
Like most of those whose lives
It decorated
For one brief glorious night,
So long ago
When I believed
Our family was for ever.

The Physics of Timelessness

"What has your wisdom revealed to you
of the vastness of things and the
eternity of the human soul?"

And suddenly the whole room was alive with
Vibrant plans, ideas, deductions, quotes
Music.
Eliot and Plato met again, Bertrand Russell
Joked with Whitehead and Bernal
While Richard Feynman played accompaniment.

From the sofa, Krishnamurti argued in Socratic fashion
That only through self-knowledge can one
Find freedom from mundane, restricting passions
And Plato, naturally, chipped in,
Saying that's what his Academy was all about.

And then, inscribed in a dull book of even duller
                                                English Extracts
My father's youthful script spoke out,

> *If I could ride upon some winged horse*
> *to that lonely cave at the foot of*
> *a mighty cliff wherein dwells . . .*
> *And if I could gain admittance to*
> *his presence; I would ask of him:–*
> *"What has your wisdom revealed to you*
> *of the vastness of things and the*
> *eternity of the (human) soul?"*

We all sighed with one mighty breath
While, quietly, in an all-embracing corner, my uncle
Wrote his war-time story, *No Land of Milk and Honey,*

Even then aware that he was destined
For the priesthood, while my father would become
                            a wild and inspired physicist.

I paused in this so wonderful party – *the vastness of things and
the eternity of the soul* – to refresh my glass and lit upon
a folded paper concealed within a book of Differential
                                        Calculus
– a recent invitation, unanswered, I imagined,
to give a paper on 'consciousness in all its aspects'

and then I came upon my brother's copy of *Agricola*
                purchased, I saw, two years before his death
and annotated by my father – *p.99 (MIND)*

And all around towers of physics books of an
                          incomprehensible beauty – and
Somewhere there the Second Law of Thermodynamics,
Schrödinger's *What is Life?* and
The Time Reversal and Refutation Theories that maybe held us
                                 in the

Now
Together in this room

But tomorrow

Tomorrow will be just memories and books,
Awful packing cases and cruel emptiness

                          But will it?

What about *page ninety-nine*
Where Tacitus says, and my father strongly underlines,
    ... the essence of man's mind is something everlasting, ... ?

~~~

The Pattern of the Real
poem for the turning of the year

And what remains
    what remains
Of those unforgettable experiences
You already are forgetting?

The performances, discussions
Meetings, agonising partings
The piercing, overwhelming insights
When the dull façades of common life
Fade from common view
And your real eye sees
The wondrous essence burning through
                the chains of time?

All that was in essence nothing
Fades to nothing
But those true experiences
Which have their source in heaven –
The magic rain-blessed kiss
            in the darkening London square
The voice of seers from yellowed pages
            in the fire-lit comforting room
The sudden stabbing recognition
       in a painting or the haunting voice of music
An animal's pure beauty
The gentle all-embracing smile of love

These remain
Distilled through and beyond succession's deadening bonds
Glowing like a constant flame
       whilst the dross falls back into the
       hollow grasp of Time
       and is as nothing.

~~~